Heal Your Self

A CBT Approach to
Reducing Therapist
Distress &
Increasing
Therapeutic
Effectiveness

John W. Ludgate

Professional Resource Press
Sarasota, Florida

Published by
Professional Resource Press
(An imprint of Professional Resource Exchange, Inc.)
Post Office Box 3197 • Sarasota, FL 34230-3197
Printed in the United States of America
Copyright © 2012 by Professional Resource Exchange, Inc.
All rights reserved

This publication is sold with the understanding that the publisher is not engaged in rendering professional services. If legal, psychological, medical, accounting, or other expert advice or assistance is sought or required, the reader should seek the services of a competent professional.

Cover and text designed by Laurie Girsch.

Library of Congress Cataloging-in-Publication Data

Ludgate, John W., date.
  Heal your self : a CBT approach to reducing therapist distress & increasing therapeutic effectiveness / John W. Ludgate.
      p. cm.
  Includes bibliographical references.
  ISBN 978-1-56887-127-1 (1-56887-127-9 : alk paper)
  1. Cognitive therapy. 2. Burn out (Psychology)--Prevention. I. Title.
  RC489.C63L82 2012
  616.89'1425--dc23
                                        2011048222

DEDICATION

To the memory of
Fred Wright, CBT mentor and friend;
and with thanks to Conor and Leslie.

TABLE OF CONTENTS

INTRODUCTION

Despite a general acknowledgement that working in the mental health field can be a source of considerable distress, a conclusion backed up by a good deal of empirical research, there are a few guidelines available for mental health practitioners, including psychotherapists, to deal with the day-to-day specific stressors encountered in this field of work. The existing literature draws largely from psychodynamic or psychoanalytic theories (Grosch & Olsen, 1994; Sedgewick, 1994). More recently, the cognitive behavior therapy literature has increasingly focused on therapists' emotional and cognitive reactions to client situations when working with more challenging clients (A. T. Beck, Freeman, & Davis, 2003; Layden et al., 1993; Leahy, 2001). However, no specific texts are dedicated specifically to the question of how Cognitive Behavior Therapy (CBT) can be systematically applied to the distress encountered by psychotherapists and other mental health professionals. Furthermore, many of the available resources in this field are focused on general issues such as "burnout" (Maslach, 1982), "compassion fatigue" (Figley, 2002), therapist renewal (Kottler, 1999), and general stress in human service professionals (Farber, 1983). As important as these topics are, the more specific transient stressors faced by mental health workers (that could lead to negative emotional, cognitive, and behavioral reactions) are rarely described and practical methods which can alleviate these problems have not been outlined in the literature. This text will focus on using the principles and practice of CBT — an empirically supported treatment for a range of problems (Butler et al., 2006) — for reducing therapist distress and the associated blunting of therapeutic effectiveness.

THE EXTENT OF THE PROBLEM

It is widely considered that working in the helping professionals, especially mental health, can frequently lead to negative consequences. These can run on a continuum from transient incidents of emotional upset or frustration with resulting behavioral consequences to a more generalized set of characteristic feelings, attitudes, and behaviors that are often labeled as "burnout." This term was first introduced by Maslach (1982). Maslach described it as a collection of symptoms including emotional exhaustion, depersonalization, and reduced personal accomplishment that occurs among individuals who professionally engage in helping people.

The incidence of such reactions is significant. Mental health specialists have been found to be at high risk for burnout (Onyett, Pillinger, & Muijen, 1997). Some professional groups appear even more at risk than others. Evans et al. (2006) found that mental health social workers show levels of stress and emotional exhaustion that are twice that of psychiatrists and three times that of the general population. Burnout levels of up to 40% have been reported in U.S. psychologists (Fortener, 1990). Results from surveys in the United Kingdom found British clinical psychologists displayed even higher levels of emotional exhaustion, depersonalization, and reduced personal accomplishment (the three components of burnout) compared to their U.S. colleagues. In addition, it was found that personal doubt was a key stressor, which appeared to correlate with burnout. Looking at indices of distress reactions less severe than burnout, Cushway and Tyler (1994) found in a survey of British clinical psychologists that 29.4% were "highly stressed."

There is good deal of research on possible predictors of stress reactions in mental health professionals. Evans et al. (2006) report that high job demand and not being valued for what one does are predictors of mental health workers' burnout. Shinn et al. (1984) reported that a source of dissatisfaction or stress was the lack of positive reinforcement or recognition for good work, which was reported by 44% of mental health professionals. Other sources of stress reported by a large number of mental health workers were feelings of inadequacy relative to one's own expectations, feeling pressure to cure clients, conflicts with other staff, and problems with clients (especially those who are emotionally demanding or those who failed to improve). Moore and Cooper (1996) also point out that, beyond the demands made by clients or organizations, the demands or expectations which mental health professionals place on themselves are also an important predictor of burnout. It has been found that certain personality types are more likely to experience stress and burnout. For example, the Type A behavior pattern — which is associated with being excessively time-conscious, competitive, ambitious, and hard driving — has been found to be a predictor of burnout (Rees & Cooper, 1992).

Research has also indicated that the longer individuals had worked in the mental health field the less successful they felt with their clients (Pines & Maslach, 1978). The same researchers also found that the higher the percentage of chronic patients in an individual's caseload, the less job satisfaction was experienced. The length of time individuals had worked in the field was also a predictor of burnout. It has also been found that longer or more advanced training was also a predictor of burnout.

The following factors have also been found to predict therapist strain or distress: emergency calls, interruptions in family life, difficulty dividing time between spouse/family and clients, and unrealistic expectations and overresponsibility for clients (Moore & Cooper, 1996).

The table below lists some of the possible factors involved in distress or burnout in mental health professionals, taken from research and anecdotal accounts from psychotherapists.

Predictors of Distress in Mental Health Professionals

Individual Characteristics	• Work for organizations • Length of time in job • More training
Personality of Professional	• Type A personality • Unrealistic expectations • Rigid, overly concerned with details • Inability to balance work and home life • Lack of confidence • Social anxiety

Predictors of Distress in Mental Health Professionals *(Cont'd)*

Client Factors
- High caseload
- Client's rights issues
- Personality disordered or chronic clients
- Aggression in clients
- Client dependency
- Demanding clients
- Uncontrollable situations

Organizational Factors
- Staff conflict
- Job overload/Time pressure
- Role ambiguity
- Lack of support from supervisor
- Poor recognition of effort
- Physical working conditions

SIGNS OF POSSIBLE STRESS/BURNOUT IN MENTAL HEALTH PRACTITIONERS

At the extreme level (which is equivalent to "burnout") where an individual is clearly impaired, the following indices of distress might be seen:

PHYSICAL/SOMATIC PROBLEMS

- Chronic fatigue/not sleeping
- Headaches
- Susceptibility to infection/compromised autoimmune system
- Appetite disturbance
- Gastrointestinal disorders (ulcers, colitis)
- Muscle tension
- Physiological symptoms of anxiety (palpitations, restlessness)

EMOTIONAL PROBLEMS

- Depression
- Anxiety
- Anger and irritability
- Frustration

BEHAVIORAL PROBLEMS

- Reduced work productivity
- Working longer yet accomplishing less
- Clock watching
- Chronic tardiness
- Avoidance of work
- Frequent complaining
- Impatience and irritable behavior directed at clients/colleagues/ family
- Mechanistic responding to clients
- Withdrawal from others
- Lack of separation of professional and social life
- Behavior related to a compulsive work ethic

COGNITIVE/ATTITUDINAL PROBLEMS

- Poor concentration
- Rigidity in thinking
- Difficulty making decisions
- Pessimism about work, clients, and life
- Cynicism towards clients and others
- Hypercritical attitude towards others
- Guilt and self-blame
- Sense of failure
- Distrust of others
- Boredom
- Grandiosity
- Sense of self-righteousness

At a milder and less impairing level, where the distress may be more situational or transient and possibly related to encountering specific stressors (client-related or organizational), all of the above may occur but for a briefer period (or episodically). A key determinant of how significant and problematic these indicators of distress are is to ascertain if any of the above represent a departure from the individual's baseline functioning. For example, a therapist who normally sleeps well and has a good sense of humor might now experience insomnia and rarely laughs at anything. A medical screening may be helpful in the event of many of these being in the physical arena to ensure that this is stress-related and not of organic etiology.

The following checklist may be a quick screening for work-related distress and indicate that issues related to the onset and maintenance of this level of stress may need to be addressed.

- ❏ Feeling tired frequently

- ❏ Arguing with others over minor things

- ❏ Never being able to relax

- ❏ Constantly feeling in demand or under pressure

- ❏ Lack of patience or tolerance

- ❏ Feeling there is not enough time for oneself, family, or friends

- ❏ Memory and concentration lapses

- ❏ Lack of interest in or time for socializing or engaging in recreational activities

- ❏ Feeling irritable, tired, and unfulfilled at the end of the work day

A COGNITIVE BEHAVIORAL MODEL OF DISTRESS IN THERAPISTS

The Cognitive model (A. T. Beck et al., 1979) theorizes that (a) cognitive events and processes significantly influence emotions and behavior, (b) perception and cognition mediate the effects of situations with regard to emotional and behavioral consequences, and (c) modification of cognition leads to emotional and behavioral change. This model, which has been demonstrated to be effective in helping a variety of client groups (such as mood and anxiety disorders), should also be reflexive. Specifically, it should apply equally to the therapist and to the client. Similarly, practitioners of mindfulness and acceptance approaches in psychotherapy (Wilson, 2008) have argued that these approaches are equally valuable and effective for the therapist and for the client. The extension of the CBT model to professionals, especially mental health practitioners, can be seen in the diagram below.

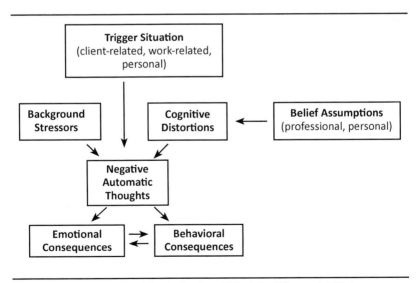

Figure 1. A Cognitive Behavioral Model of Therapist Distress

A more detailed analysis of the components of the model, as applied to therapists in distress, is outlined below.

TRIGGER SITUATIONS

The triggers (situations which can precipitate emotional and behavioral reactions) for mental health practitioners may include (a) client or therapy-related events and/or (b) other work-related situations (organizational or administrative).

Examples of these triggers in the first case can include the following:

- Dealing with a very demanding client who makes frequent requests for extra emergency sessions or telephones regularly in crisis
- Working with a highly suicidal or hopeless client
- Attempting to do therapy with a "resistant" client who challenges the therapist every step of the way
- Working with emotionally charged issues in a client, such as child sexual abuse, rape, or violence

Examples of other work-related stressors might include:

- Being overwhelmed by paperwork
- Being assigned too many cases or a large number of difficult cases
- Role conflict or role ambiguity
- Interpersonal conflict at work
- Professional isolation

BACKGROUND STRESSORS

Background stressors, which might lower the threshold for emotional and cognitive reactions in particular situations, can involve any events inside or outside work (e.g., a change of job, an increase in work hours, family problems, and financial difficulties).

BELIEFS

This refers to general assumptions, rules, or beliefs that individuals adopt, and which profoundly influence how experiences are viewed and interpreted.

Key dysfunctional beliefs relating to work as a therapist or mental professional might include:

- I have to be successful with all my clients all the time.
- I must always have good sessions with my clients.
- I should not dislike any of my clients.
- I should not feel any negative emotions related to clients or therapy.
- I should not ask for advice or support from colleagues or get professional help myself.
- My clients should always respect and like me.
- People I try to help should not be difficult and resistant.
- If I extend myself to help clients, they ought to be motivated to change and reward me for my efforts.

More general dysfunctional beliefs relating to work might include:

- I must always be completely competent and in control.
- It is terrible to be criticized or disapproved of.
- Life in the workplace should be fair and just.
- My worth as a person is dependent on my job performance.

COGNITIVE DISTORTIONS

Cognitive distortions are information processing biases or thinking errors that are influenced by beliefs and generate negative automatic thoughts. In mental health practice, the following distortions might be seen:

- All or nothing thinking: Seeing things as black or white. For example, the therapist thinks he is a total failure as a therapist based on the fact that some clients are not improving.

- Overgeneralizing: One negative event is seen as a general pattern. For example, an assumption is made by the therapist that since one of his clients is unhappy with his treatment, then none of his clients are satisfied with the therapy he is providing.
- Mental filter: Seeing only the negative aspects of a situation and filtering out the positives. For example, the therapist sees only the fact that a client has had a setback and fails to recognize how stable the client has been recently and how effectively the setback was handled by the individual.
- Mind reading: Assuming one knows what someone is thinking. For example, when a client fails to keep an appointment, the therapist assumes that the client thinks that the therapy or therapist is unhelpful.

AUTOMATIC THOUGHTS

Automatic thoughts are specific thoughts, images, or memories related to a specific precipitating situation and often reflexive in nature. These can be negative in tone and often will have adverse emotional consequences. Negative automatic thoughts related to a specific client situation might include the following:

- There is no progress.
- I am not helping this client at all.
- If the client is angry or critical, I am not handling things properly.
- He is resisting me and doesn't want to change or improve.
- This person's situation is so realistically terrible that there is nothing I can do to help.
- I get all the difficult cases like this one.

Automatic thoughts experienced by therapists related to nonclient situations might include the following:

- My supervisor or colleagues are completely unsupportive of me.
- I will never get this paperwork done.
- Everybody is dumping on me.

- Why do I bother when I get so few rewards, financial or otherwise?

EMOTIONAL AND BEHAVIORAL REACTIONS

Emotional reactions may include anger, frustration, anxiety, irritability, sadness, and dysphoria. Behavioral reactions may involve a range of unhealthy or maladaptive behaviors to deal with the stress encountered with clients or work in general. These may include:

- Working longer and longer hours
- Isolating oneself from family, friends, and colleagues
- Overeating, drinking, or using drugs

In addition, there may be a tendency to act or behave towards the clients in a way that becomes antitherapeutic and involves a poor standard of care, such as:

- Withdrawing from the client in session
- Becoming much less active in session
- Providing support rather than the more problem-focused therapy the therapist customarily practices
- Displaying irritable behavior towards the client
- Procrastination expressed by not returning phone calls and being chronically late for sessions

EXAMPLES OF THERAPIST REACTIONS

In the next several pages, a number of examples of how this model can explain therapists' reactions will be given.

EXAMPLE 1

Several years ago I had a "light bulb" moment related to my professional life, which demonstrated clearly the critical role which cognitions can play in the distress experienced in working as a mental health professional. I was attending a workshop on Cognitive Re-Appraisal Therapy, one of a number of cognitive behavioral models. I volunteered to be a client in a role-play with the presenter. I was instructed to think of a recent experience involving a negative emotional shift. The previous day I had learned that a client of mine, who I had been seeing in therapy for over a year, had had a major relapse and had been hospitalized. I was still experiencing some distress concerning this development. When I described the situation (the client's relapse and subsequent hospitalization) to "my therapist" (the presenter), the following interchange took place:

Therapist:	What feelings do you have about this situation?
Me:	Guilt, anxiety.
Therapist:	What thoughts are you having about this situation? What does it mean to you?
Me:	That my therapy wasn't successful.
Therapist:	And if that was true, what would that mean?
Me:	That I am not a good therapist.
Therapist:	And if that were true, what would that mean?
Me:	That I am inadequate.
Therapist:	As a therapist?
Me:	Yes, and as a person too.

The therapist then went back and summarized the chain of assumptions implicit in my moving from the factual knowledge that my client had relapsed to my belief that I was inadequate as a person. These were:

If this client has relapsed, then my therapy was not successful.
If my therapy was not successful, then I am not a good therapist.
If I am not a good therapist, then I am inadequate as a person.

I was startled to discover how irrational and dysfunctional my thinking was, especially since I was a practicing Cognitive Therapist who helped my clients daily with their irrational thoughts! That obviously did not automatically protect me from having irrational and dysfunctional thoughts myself. In addition, I had always seen myself as a therapist who was well adjusted, did not get overly involved emotionally, lost perspective, or had unrealistic expectations regarding myself and my clients. Since this "wake up call," I have made it a point to closely monitor my own cognitions and feelings in therapy situations. Furthermore, in supervising novice therapists, I have encouraged them to examine their own cognitive and emotional effects of the therapeutic impasses or difficulties. They are further urged to use cognitive interventions on their own distorted thinking, which is often linked to negative emotional reactions, as the cognitive behavioral model would predict.

In the example given above, one can see the complex interaction of trigger situations, cognitive events, and negative feelings. There are clearly a number of levels of cognition involved in the overall reaction. Specifically, there are:

- Negative automatic thoughts related to the situation of the client relapse ("This therapy wasn't successful")
- Cognitive distortions or information processing biases which, in this example, included mental filter and personalization
- Dysfunctional beliefs that included (a) professional beliefs ("I am not a good therapist") and (b) personal beliefs ("I am inadequate")

This example fits with the Cognitive Model presented previously (Figure 1, p. 7) and illustrates it in a clear and understandable way. The other components in Figure 1 are Behavior and Background Stress. The cognitive and emotional reactions outlined in the previous example might have also led to behaviors such as the provision of inferior therapy, attempts to overcompensate by doing too much for other clients, or maladaptive behavior outside of work (such as overeating, irritability, and withdrawal). Background stress, such as concerns and worries related to health and family, could have also lowered the threshold for dysfunctional responding, both emotional and cognitively.

EXAMPLE 2

It may be helpful to imagine yourself being in the following hypothetical situation. A client is referred to you by a colleague who notes that the client may have some "borderline tendencies." Preparing for your first interview with this new client, you might notice some feelings of anxiety or irritation possibly linked to negative thoughts, such as "The client will be very angry, will be difficult to treat, will be resistant, and challenge me at every step. It is not fair that I get all the difficult cases." These automatic thoughts might in turn be subtended by underlying beliefs such as "Clients should always treat me well, be compliant, and easy" or "Life in the workplace should be fair." As a result of the emotional and cognitive reactions described above, your behavior toward the client might be different from your normal therapy behavior in that you may be more distant, act defensively, or become overly vigilant with this client. These behaviors may in turn trigger some "borderline" or antitherapeutic behavior in the client if he or she perceives you to be uncaring, nontrustworthy, or disinterested. This set of thoughts and expectations can have both a damaging effect on the therapy itself and trigger a lot of pre-emptive distress in the therapist. Challenging and modifying such thoughts to something like "I will have to wait and see what, if any, borderline features this client has; in the meantime I will concentrate on my two goals for this first session: to identify problems and targets and to develop initial rapport with the client." This would both reduce the anxiety and irritation experienced and facilitate more effective therapy.

EXAMPLE 3

In my own clinical practice, the following example demonstrates the dual processing that can occur while interacting with clients during therapy sessions. Specifically, they are

1. the overt interaction that occurs between the therapist and the client; and
2. the covert processes of the therapist (which may involve experiencing a number of feelings and thoughts) which the therapist has to deal with while at the same time responding appropriately and therapeutically to the client.

Some time ago, I provided therapy to a young woman whose stated goal for therapy was to rid herself of frequent and severe panic attacks. The first several sessions were spent doing standard cognitive behavioral assessment and intervention (Wells, 1997). She was educated about the vicious cycle of panic and instructed in a number of interventions which could help break the panic cycle (decatastrophizing her frightening thoughts, reattribution of the sensations she experienced to anxiety rather than to a heart condition, and breathing retraining). At the beginning of the 4th session I asked her how she had fared over the previous week and, specifically, how many panic attacks she had had in the intervening period. She excitedly told me that she had been panic-free during that time. I inquired if she had used the techniques we had worked on and if this had in fact led to this positive outcome. I should note that my mood at his time was one of mild elation, as I was anticipating that she would, in fact, tell me that the CBT interventions had been the key factor in her panic-free week. Instead, she said, "Actually, none of those things worked, so I gave them up, but I remembered cutting myself years ago when I was angry and I did that again and it worked like a charm. So I now have a way of controlling the panic attacks."

My emotional state quickly changed to acute anxiety complete with a number of associated physiological symptoms and the following instantaneous automatic thoughts: "Oh, no. She's probably borderline. Therapy is going to be a struggle. There will be rages, drama, dependency, and volatile behavior." I struggled with these internal (cognitive) reactions, as I tried to remain calm outwardly. I responded by saying, "I am glad you haven't had any panic attacks but I'd like us to look at the pros and cons of that strategy as a means of controlling the attacks, if you are OK with that." While saying this, my heart was beating fast and I felt some perspiration on my face and the beginning of a headache. I used a brief applied relaxation technique on myself to deal with my physical anxiety. In addition, I did some Cognitive Therapy on myself, responding to my initial anxiety-provoking thoughts by rational responses such as "This doesn't mean she has all the characteristics of a borderline; she may just be an occasional cutter. I should wait and see. She's been fine about boundaries, and so on, thus far. Maybe that's a good sign."

In this example, the therapist is simultaneously conducting CBT with a client, while doing CBT on himself in response to a therapy incident. I know this process has occurred many times in my daily practice and every therapist can probably identify with this and similar scenarios.

It is important that therapists learn to emotionally "take care of themselves" by developing skills to detect and deal with the emotional challenges faced every day in their field. In doing so, not only will their levels of emotional distress be less, but also they will in all likelihood be better therapists, as it appears obvious that such reactions can interfere with the provision of effective treatment. The rest of this text will offer some practical tools to assist therapists in reducing stress and distress in the mental health workplace.

CONCEPTUALIZATION OF DISTRESS IN MENTAL HEALTH PROVIDERS

A number of different issues can contribute to distress reactions of mental health professionals. The confluence of factors, which may predict distress in a particular individual at a particular time, will now be examined. It is hypothesized that the following factors will play a role in the development of the negative emotional and behavioral outcomes described previously:

- Situational triggers at work, including both client-related and non-client-related work stressors
- Personal characteristics of the therapist/mental health provider
- Expectations and beliefs of the therapist/mental health provider
- Personal coping style, skills, and resources of the individual
- Levels of non-work stress
- The degree to which the professional training received equips the individual to deal with these stressors
- The presence or absence of staff support systems to reduce or alleviate these problems

Using the above analysis we could predict maximum levels of distress where a therapist:

- Has a large case load with many challenging clients
- Has unrealistic beliefs regarding these clients, therapy, or himself/herself as a therapist
- Works in a very autocratic agency that makes many demands on the therapist but provides little staff support and fails to prioritize staff satisfaction or fulfillment

- Has received little or no training in coping with the emotional reactions triggered by working with certain client groups
- Has little emotional resilience and poor problem-solving or coping skills.
- Has a great deal of additional non-work stress in his or her life

Conversely, we might expect that low levels of stress would be found in therapists who have few of the above factors present. Successful interventions and preventative efforts to reduce distress should target each of these areas. Specifically, the following may become targets for intervention:

- Reducing or better managing client-related and other work stressors
- Modifying and revising dysfunctional beliefs and expectations of therapists
- Facilitating better agency support and supervision for individuals dealing with challenging clients
- Encouraging and promoting better training for therapists in management of their own emotional reactions
- Helping to develop better coping resources and problem-solving skills leading to a greater sense of self-efficacy

In subsequent sections of this text, methods to achieve these goals will be described. First, each of the above factors, which can have a major impact on therapists or mental health providers, will be described and discussed.

CLIENT-RELATED STRESSORS

Stress reactions, including severe emotional and behavioral reactions, can occur with certain types of clients or critical incidents involving clients. These reactions can occur at different times within or outside the therapy session. The therapist, for example, can have distress triggered by client behavior in session but distress can also be experienced before or after sessions when thinking about these clients and their problems or behaviors. Most therapists will have the experience that certain names on a list of clients scheduled for a particular day can elicit strong internal reactions. To illustrate, consider the example of a client with a personality disorder. First, the therapist may have a sense of foreboding or apprehension realizing this client is due in for a session shortly. Second, during the ensuing session the therapist may experience irritation, anxiety, or hopelessness when it appears that the therapy session is going nowhere, especially if the client is perceived to be "responsible" for this by not participating in the session or by not following through with homework assignments. Later, the therapist may feel frustrated and annoyed after (a) reading a feedback form filled out by the client indicating dissatisfaction with the therapy or the therapist, or (b) recalling a remark made by the client in session that was critical or challenging.

In addition to the above, the following client populations or therapy situations may put therapists at risk of some level of emotional distress.

CHRONICALLY DEPRESSED CLIENTS

Any therapist who has had experience working with individuals with long histories of chronic, unremitting depression can attest to how challenging working with this kind of client can be. These clients are likely to show little evidence of improvement over the short term and in some cases may be critical of therapy or aggressive in their hope-lessness. This can lead to the therapist feeling anxious, frustrated, or hopeless with associated thoughts such as "I have nothing to offer here" or "This person will never change." Emery (2000) warns of the danger of what he describes as becoming the "frustrated satisfier" with these clients, where the therapist believes he or she *has* to satisfy the client or *must* get him better. This is likely to end up with frustration for both the therapist and client. The key is to *want* to get the client better but not to *need* this from the client or for oneself. It is also important, as Emery points out, to focus on the process rather than on the outcome. These clients may be making some small and gradual steps that represent progress, such as spending less time in bed, but these are overlooked because the therapist and client are thinking in more global terms and being frustrated that the depression itself has not been eliminated. The demoralization and hopelessness of these clients can "rub off" on therapists who come to believe that this client's situation is, in fact, hopeless. They can then inadvertently communicate this to the client. It is important to maintain a problem-solving attitude and to recognize the cognitive distortions present in this form of thinking (all-or-nothing thinking, catastrophizing). It is also important that the therapist and client share realistic goals. Given a history of chronic or recurrent depression, a more realistic goal would be to improve coping and reduce both depressive symptoms and the degree of impairment in function associated with depression, rather than the elimination of all depressive symptoms permanently — a goal which would likely set up the therapist and client for a future failure experience.

SUICIDAL CLIENTS

The probability that a mental health specialist will have to deal with a client's attempted or successful suicide is quite high, considering the elevated risk in clients who are depressed and hopeless, or have chronic, unremitting, and untreatable pain. Any therapist who has had the experience of a client committing suicide during or after therapy can attest to the emotional impact such an event can have. I encountered this early in my career as a psychotherapist. I recall vividly the shock, anxiety, guilt, and sadness I felt on hearing the news of one of my clients. She was a young nurse with severe Torticollis, and who was unable to practice in the field that had become her identity due to the severity of her medical condition, and had taken a huge overdose and died. I ruminated endlessly about what I could have done differently, what I had missed, and how I could have protected or saved her. This is probably the supreme test of a therapist's resilience, given the possibility of self-blame and feelings of helplessness and inadequacy.

Unsuccessful suicide attempts by current clients can also be very emotionally arousing for the therapist. These attempts at suicide can lead to feelings of frustration, anxiety, anger, or sadness with associated thoughts that may have themes of incompetence, helplessness, unfairness, or blame toward the client. Decisions about safety are often very difficult and draining. Hospitalization, while ensuring short-term safety, is often no more than a short-term solution and the worry about safety may continue or be increased on discharge when the client is often now energized and feeling somewhat better. In addition, there is the issue of the relative merits of protecting individuals from themselves versus the therapeutic consequences of involuntary hospitalization in terms of trust issues. It should, of course, be pointed out that good clinical and ethical practice makes safety more important than any other concerns and, in reality, clients may not react negatively in the long term to the therapist taking unilateral action in such a situation. Every time a highly suicidal individual leaves a therapist's office, the situation is rife with continuing concern and anxiety until the next appointment. The awareness of the medico-legal issues involved in working with suicidal clients may take an emotional toll as well. Certain individuals, often those diagnosed with a personality disorder, may flaunt their suicidality verbally or behaviorally in a highly manipulative way. With such clients, there may be a mixture of anger (due to the sense of being manipulated) and anxiety (based on the realization that, for all the manipulative behavior involved, the individual may deliberately or accidentally succeed). Other chronically depressed clients may be aggressively hopeless with the potential for suicide being enduring and unchanging. With these individuals, they may again have mixed feelings of frustration that they are not amenable to therapy and anxiety that they may act on their hopelessness.

HIGHLY ANXIOUS CLIENTS

Individuals who usually have a long history of anxiety symptoms, and who are overwhelmed by these feelings, can be a significant challenge for therapists who feel that symptom-relief is urgent and necessary.

Koepping (1998) describes a case of significant countertransferential anxiety while treating a highly anxious woman who was unable to remain in therapy sessions for longer than 15 to 20 minutes due to her ever-increasing anxiety during each session. The therapist in this case began to feel very inadequate because she could not immediately or quickly reduce this level of anxiety and thereby facilitate the client remaining for the entire session. She began to realize that she was personalizing this situation and taking too much responsibility for the therapeutic progress or lack of it. This cognitive shift led to more effective therapy. In cases such as the above, it can be seen that the therapist's implicit beliefs come into play in the reactions of impatience, anxiety, or frustration. It is often helpful to examine these assumptions when the trigger situation eliciting the therapist discomfort is the client's high level of affect. The assumptions may include the beliefs "I should be able to stop this" and "If it continues like this, something terrible will happen." These assumptions can then be challenged using standard cognitive behavioral techniques, as will be described later. Lastly, the therapist may also need to utilize some anxiety-management or self-regulation skills on himself or herself, as well as challenging the unrealistic beliefs behind the anxiety or frustration experienced.

HOMICIDAL CLIENTS

A highly provocative situation, in terms of its potential for therapist distress, is learning that a current client has recently or in the past killed someone. Two challenging situations related to this were encountered by the writer. These two situations involved seeing a current client's picture on the front page of the local newspaper after he had fatally shot his two brothers-in-law, and receiving a copy of a postmortem report indicating that another client whom he was treating had accidentally or deliberately killed her newborn child. Another difficult situation is when a client reports having homicidal thoughts, but it is extremely hard for the therapist to assess the actual risk to any individual who is named. Having this person detained involuntarily may reduce the homicide risk but jeopardize the therapy relationship.

ANGRY CLIENTS

These clients can create a great challenge for therapists. If the client has a history of aggressive or violent behavior, there may be a realistic general fear that this person may hurt someone including the therapist, and there is often an understandable specific anxiety regarding safety if the patient's anger is escalating very quickly and intensely in session. A number of therapists have been assaulted and even killed by clients, so this anxiety is well-founded in some cases. Other issues that could arise include the therapist believing that it is up to him or her to calm this person before something bad happens. There may be a worry that any form of confrontation may trigger an escalation in anger. In addition, there may be a concern that colleagues in adjoining rooms will be upset or disturbed by the patient's behavior. Levinson (1998) describes the countertransference involved in the treatment of a difficult client who was angry about everything and how this was handled. Matsakis (1998) describes the many ways that anger can manifest itself in therapy and ways of judging the potential for clients crossing the line from anger into violent behavior. It is important that the anger is understood from a thorough case conceptualization, which examines the cognitive, emotional, and behavioral components of the anger response. Beliefs underlying anger which clients might subscribe to can include the following: "People will hurt me if I am not on guard," "I am vulnerable," "I better strike first before this person does," or "Everyone is out to take advantage of me." These assumptions can be the focus of cognitive behavioral interventions. In the presence of an angry client, therapists may have the following cognitions associated with their own emotions of anxiety or frustration: "They have no right to act that way towards me" or "I must control this or it will get dangerous." These cognitions and feelings need also to be addressed in order to facilitate a reduction in the therapist's distress and to maximize the effectiveness of therapy.

PERSONALITY DISORDERED CLIENTS

Any clinician who has worked with individuals with severe personality disorder (e.g., paranoid, borderline, or narcissistic clients) can attest to the fact that this can be very stressful and challenging. There are many behaviors and beliefs in these individuals' repertoires which can become triggered by the therapy process leading to both transference and countertransference reactions. While certain nonimpairing negative emotional reactions to these behaviors are normal and to be expected, therapists faced with such therapeutic roadblocks may also engage in some counterproductive and dysfunctional thinking patterns.

In their ground-breaking volume *Cognitive Therapy of Personality Disorders*, A. T. Beck et al. (2006) describe how in the treatment of personality disorders the patient and the therapist's dysfunctional beliefs may interact in dysfunctional ways. For example, the client's belief that everything is hopeless may be shared by the therapist who has "bought into" the patient's pessimism and demoralization. Another way in which the therapist may act antitherapeutically is by colluding in the setting of highly unrealistic goals (the patient will never be depressed again), which sets the client up for a sense of failure given that certain individuals do have a high risk for relapse. Additionally, therapists working with personality-disordered clients may become frustrated by the slow or minimal progress being made, which again may be unrealistic given the long-term nature and duration of these problems.

Leahy (2001) suggests that in working with challenging clients, including those with personality disorders, therapists themselves may fall into the trap of using the same cognitive distortions that they often elicit and modify in their clients. The therapist may describe the client as resistant, which is an example of Labeling; the therapist believes the client will never get any better, which involves Fortune Telling;

or there is an assumption by the therapist that the client has not made any improvement, which indicates possible All-or-Nothing Thinking. Leahy gives many other examples of how therapists can engage in these cognitive biases. He also describes a sequence that can occur, when working with certain clients, where the therapist experiences a number of negative emotions triggered by these clients' behaviors in session. These feelings will often have associated negative thoughts which are based in part on implicit rules or beliefs of the therapist. These might include a feeling of anger with an associated thought such as "He is selfish and doesn't appreciate what I am doing for him." Underlying this may be an implicit rule that the therapist follows, such as "People should be fair and reciprocate."

In another client situation, a therapist may feel some demoralization with an associated thought such as "there is nothing I can do to help this patient." Again, the therapist may have an underlying implicit rule which might be "I am a failure if I don't have all the answers."

A. T. Beck et al. (2006) and Layden et al. (1993) point out that therapists, in working with clients with Borderline Personality Disorder in particular, will often have strong emotional reactions triggered by these clients' therapy-interfering behaviors (self-sabotage, noncompliance with homework, risk-taking behaviors). At such times, it is important that the therapist look at his or her own underlying thoughts, assumptions, and beliefs. For example, it would be worthwhile to check out the assumption that the client has malicious intentions or malevolent motivation for certain anti-therapeutic behaviors or "doesn't want to get better." Instead, consideration should be given to a number of different attributions or explanations, such as the client's fear of the implications of change and belief that "the devil you know is better that the one you don't." It could be predicted that steps toward change may represent something that is unfamiliar and hence provoke anxiety for the client, if the therapist identifies an underlying belief such as "I won't know who I am if I change." Trying to conceptualize the function the behavior has from the client's own viewpoint (e.g., how does it fit with their basic belief about themselves, others, or the world?) may be very helpful in preventing a therapeutic impasse and also serve to reduce therapist frustration. Layden and colleagues (1993) enumerate some characteristic automatic thoughts of therapists, when faced with borderline patients' outbursts or irrational demands. These might include "There is nothing I can do to help this patient," "This is a career patient

I am dealing with and I'd only needlessly be banging my head against a wall to work with him," "This is the kind of patient who could bad mouth or sue me. I had better stay as passive and uninvolved as possible," or "I must be tough and detached to prove that I cannot easily be manipulated." All of the above responses can have a detrimental effect on both the therapy process and on the therapist's affective/cognitive and behavioral reactions. Therapists need to be alert to the possibility that they themselves will have dysfunctional thinking patterns triggered by the challenges presented by personality-disordered clients.

TRAUMA SURVIVORS

The negative effects on therapists working with individuals who have been traumatized have been recognized in the professional literature. Conducting therapy with clients who have severe Posttraumatic Stress Disorder (PTSD) or working professionally with clients with histories of sexual abuse can lead to a variety of emotional reactions. These emotional reactions can range from overidentification, leading to a loss of objectivity; or to the opposite end of the spectrum where therapists (who have had prolonged exposure to such cases) lose their ability to empathize, become cynical, develop "burn out," and deliver therapy in a mechanical and superficial manner.

A syndrome called Compassion Fatigue (also known as Secondary Traumatic Stress Syndrome which occurs in individuals working extensively with victims of trauma) has been described by a number of writers (Figley, 2002; Stamm, 2003). This syndrome includes a number of dysfunctional reactions on the part of caregivers, including those described earlier in this text (pp. 4-6).

In cases of abuse, especially of younger children, it is not unusual for therapists to feel a great deal of anger towards perpetrators. This can create difficulties if the perpetrator is within the family and is in some way involved in the therapy process. When working with combat-related PTSD, therapists' own views concerning the "morality" of war may be triggered. There may also be feelings of anger towards the army or government administration when clients present with enduring "psychological scars" and incapacitating problems. I can recall quite clearly the degree of distress I personally experienced in working with Vietnam veterans who described to me some of the scenes they had witnessed while on tour, including attacks on unarmed civilians which resulted in women and children being killed.

Equally, when working with victims of sexual assault where "justice was not done" in a legal sense, there may be many different emotions involved for the therapist beyond the initial compassion and empathy for the victim. Individuals working exclusively with these populations may need to develop effective methods of "looking after themselves." These methods might include supervision, setting up a staff support system, and attending workshops on topics such as Compassion Fatigue — all of which may help them realize that their reactions are to be expected and provide them with tools to deal with these feelings.

CLIENTS WITH LOW FRUSTRATION TOLERANCE OR HIGH LEVELS OF AVOIDANCE

These two issues will be dealt with together, as clients with either of these problems have in common an intolerance of negative affect, which can interfere with therapy. Clients with low frustration tolerance will generally not want to engage in therapy activities (which involve pain or frustration and will engage in certain quick-fix strategies to reduce their frustration) which can prevent the experiential exposure work necessary to promote deeper longer-term changes. Therapists may find themselves getting frustrated with the client for not "taking the risk," despite the hard work being done by the therapist helping them to see the benefits of doing so. They may become irritated that clients will not put themselves in any situations, which creates temporary discomfort in the service of eventual progress and change. There may be a tendency to blame or criticize the client for this avoidance rather than to examine the beliefs which lead to this behavior, such as "I won't be able to tolerate these feelings" or "I will lose control."

In addition, confrontation is unlikely to work with these clients and following the theory underlying Motivational Interviewing (Miller & Rollnick, 2002), clients will only be motivated to change this behavior if they see the benefits of doing so. The advantages of continuing with old habits need to be perceived as outweighed by the advantages of the new course of action. The therapist's task is to facilitate this realization rather than become embroiled in the "blaming game." The stages of change model of Prochaska and DiClemente (1984) can be very useful with all of these challenging cases as a means of understanding so called "resistance." As well as being of proven effectiveness therapeutically, the motivational interviewing approach can also help reduce a good deal of therapist frustration and irritation.

Many clients seen in clinical practice are avoidant in many different aspects of their functioning (behaviorally, affectively, and cognitively). This is usually a long-standing strategy, which may have worked at some time or in certain situations in their lives, but which now creates problems. When faced with homework assignments or discussions of sensitive topics in therapy, the avoidance may be manifested in certain ways such as changing the subject, "forgetting" homework, or canceling appointments. Again, therapists may find themselves reacting emotionally to these incidents due in part to some mediating thoughts such as "He doesn't want to get better" or "She is doing this to deliberately obstruct possible progress." As with all therapy impasses, it is helpful to go back to the case conceptualization to determine if there are identified beliefs (e.g., "It will lead to a total loss of control if I get too anxious" or " I am a weak and incompetent person and will fail at this homework assignment") which can explain the behavior in question. The therapist can now set up interventions and behavioral experiments to test out these assumptions, rather than personalizing the reluctance and avoidance by thinking counter-therapeutic thoughts such as "She is deliberately resisting me."

OVERLY DEPENDENT CLIENTS

Working with such clients can be a source of frustration for therapists and mental health practitioners for a number of reasons. These clients may (a) be passive and inactive in therapy sessions, (b) fail to complete homework assignments, (c) expect the therapist to "cure" or solve their problems, and (d) make many extra demands on the therapist such as initiating "crisis" telephone calls to the therapist or requesting extra sessions. In addition, therapists may sometimes fall into the trap of doing too much for these clients, due to their own desire or need to be a "rescuer," which reinforces the dependent behaviors.

It is important with such clients to repeatedly stress the collaborative nature of therapy and the importance of self-efficacy and learning to "be one's own therapist." The client needs to be given more and more responsibility in therapy in conjunction with a reduction of the therapist's input, as therapy proceeds. The provision of frequent choices for the clients and a more questioning style will facilitate this collaborative team approach rather than the therapist being overly prescriptive or directive. In addition, it is helpful to explore the beliefs which underlie the dependent behaviors, such as "I am incompetent and inadequate,"

"I am unable to do this homework and will screw it up," or "I need someone more competent to do things for me since I am so useless." Challenging these beliefs, as well as attempting to promote change in dependent-type behaviors, is likely to yield better therapeutic outcomes than being frustrated by the concrete therapy-interfering manifestations of these dependent traits and associated beliefs.

POTENTIAL THERAPIST-CLIENT TRIGGER SITUATIONS AND ASSOCIATED EMOTIONAL AND COGNITIVE REACTIONS

Related to working with challenging clients, the following specific situations may also be triggers for a therapist experiencing negative emotional and cognitive reactions. These may need to be monitored and modified:

Situation 1: The client is noncompliant.
Possible therapist emotional reactions: Frustration, irritability.
Possible therapist thoughts: The patient is deliberately resisting or trying to control me. I am not a good enough therapist to get compliance.

Situation 2: The client complains about everything, including therapy.
Possible therapist emotional reactions: Anger, anxiety.
Possible therapist thoughts: He is doing this to frustrate me. I can't stand it when he does this. The client has no appreciation of what I have done for him. I am not doing a good job, as he is dissatisfied with therapy.

Situation 3: The client presents with new crises every session.
Possible therapist emotional reactions: Anxiety, frustration.
Possible thoughts: We are getting nowhere here. This person will never benefit from therapy, as there is too much going on. She is doing this to avoid looking at the deeper issues. I can't handle all of this stuff, it is too overwhelming.

It is beyond the scope of this text to discuss all client group types, which may trigger reactions in those working with them. The interested reader is referred to published resources that describe the issues and most effective methods to handle the stress involved. Included are a few references that deal with the following client populations: substance abusers (LaCoursie, 2001), AIDS/HIV patients (Miller, 2000), sexual offenders (Fisher, Houston, & Galloway, 2008), and the terminally ill (Paradis, 1987).

NONCLIENT WORK STRESSORS

In addition to clinical situations that can elicit distress, there may be a number of non-client stressors that can serve as triggers for therapist or practitioner distress. For individuals working in agencies, these might include the following:

- Too great a case load due to staff shortage
- Too little time to prepare for clients or to receive training or supervision
- Too much paperwork
- Restrictions and limits on self-determined work practice
- Unclear agency objectives or agency objectives which are at variance with those of the therapist
- Having no impact on organizational policies effecting therapy services
- Lack of reward or appreciation from the agency the therapist works for
- Lack of support/supervision when problems arise in therapy practice
- Lack of a collegial, supportive atmosphere
- Inequitable treatment of employees

For individuals working in private practice, these might include:

- Isolation from colleagues
- Long hours working alone
- Less time for recreation and family involvement
- Little support from colleagues
- No time or money for training or supervision
- Dependence on client attendance for one's income

- Concern that clients will drop out with subsequent financial ramifications
- Few referral sources
- Complicated cases with no possibility for staffing or consultation

PERSONAL CHARACTERISTICS
OF THERAPISTS

It would seem likely that there is an interaction effect between certain client or work stressors and the personality of the therapist, with both contributing to the consequences outlined earlier. Related to this is an issue which has generated interest for many years, that is, the question of what leads individuals to chose psychotherapy or counseling as a career. Does this career choice correlate with a particular type of personality? Does having certain personality traits make some therapists more vulnerable to distress or burnout? Few definitive findings have emerged from research in this area. Rees and Cooper (1992) found that the Type A personality (characterized by being driven, competitive, ambitious, and excessively time-conscious) is a predictor of burnout in mental health workers, and Moore and Cooper (1996) found that individuals who had a sense of overresponsibility for clients were more likely to experience strain or distress in doing therapy. Beyond this, it is a not clear from empirical studies what personality characteristics distinguish mental health professionals from individuals in other careers, and which characteristics of therapists might be predictive of burnout and specific distress. Nonetheless, some hypotheses have been offered in the literature regarding prevalent characteristics of therapists and amongst these are the following:

- They have a desire to help others.
- They possess a good deal of idealism.
- They are optimistic about the ability of people to change.
- They have a curiosity about human behavior.
- They feel good when they can have a positive impact on others.

If the above characteristics are rigidly held and if their current reality is at variance with these needs or wants, it is easy to see how the therapists can set themselves up for frustration, disappointment, and anxiety. Leahy (2001) theorizes that there are certain core needs, which some therapists appear to have, which motivate them. These can also be a recipe for distress when they remain unsatisfied. These needs include:

- A need for approval, respect, and admiration
- A desire for control, competence, or power
- A tendency to have excessive self-sacrifice or codependency
- A need for the reinforcement provided by emotional voyeurism
- A desire to be perfect with very high standards being set for the therapist and the client
- A need for superiority over others, which is enshrined in an all-powerful, overly directive therapist role
- An aspiration to understand oneself better through therapy and training

Clearly many of these are dysfunctional in that they will conflict with the reality of day-to-day situations faced by therapists.

BELIEF SYSTEMS OF THERAPISTS

Much of what was described in the last section can also be seen as involving cognitive content and processes, which the CBT model posits as important determining factors in emotional and behavioral problems.

The beliefs held by therapists can be broken down into three groups:

1. Beliefs or expectations concerning clients and therapy
2. Beliefs or expectations for themselves
3. More general beliefs about work

Examples of dysfunctional beliefs concerning clients and therapy might include:

- My clients should not be difficult, resistant, or challenging.
- They should work as hard as I am to make the therapy work.
- All therapy sessions should be as the textbooks describe.
- I should never be disrespected or criticized by a client.

- Clients should be motivated to change and to fully engage in therapy.
- I should be loved and admired by my clients.

Examples of dysfunctional beliefs concerning themselves, as therapists, might include:

- I must be successful with all my clients.
- If I am not successful in alleviating clients' problems, I can't feel good about myself.
- I should not dislike any of my clients.
- I must always have good judgment as a professional.
- I should have all the answers.
- I should not have any emotional reactions myself and, if I do, I should control them and never show this to clients or colleagues.

Examples of general dysfunctional attitudes about work in general might include:

- Life in the workplace should be fair and just.
- My worth as a person is dependent on my job performance.
- I must have things the way I want them.
- I will be seen as weak if I ask for help.
- Other people should see things my way.
- I must be perceived as totally competent.

It is useful to examine the underlying expectations, beliefs, and assumptions of therapists when they experience work-related distress. Thinking patterns similar to the above should be identified and then dealt with effectively using cognitive behavioral methods, as will be described later.

COPING STRATEGIES

As mentioned previously, working in the field of mental health will invariably cause some degree of distress. However, the manner in which individuals respond to work stressors may in itself produce further problems. For example, a therapist who works harder and harder or brings work home to distract himself or herself from emotional issues or uses alcohol, drugs, or overeating to deal with stress clearly is compounding the original problem. Yet many mental health practitioners, despite knowing the costs of these behaviors, engage in similar ineffective and dysfunctional coping strategies. There is a scarce amount of research on coping strategies or styles for mental health practitioners, but extrapolating from other research some assumptions can be made. First, therapists who are stressed will probably tend to fall back on a repertoire of well-learned, habitual coping strategies. These may be reinforced because they have short-term benefits, even if the long-term costs are significant. Second, some of these strategies may actually prevent effective problem solving, as they may involve distraction, avoidance, or band-aid actions.

Examples of general coping strategies that are ineffective or dysfunctional might include the following:

- Becoming compulsive about work standards
- Working longer hours to the detriment of family or social life
- Isolation
- Use of alcohol, drugs, or food to reduce distress
- Neglecting previous sources of healthy stress-reduction (exercise, hobbies, family, friends)
- Going through the motions mechanically with clients
- Providing supportive, rather than more focused, therapy
- Switching models when reaching therapeutic impasses

Later in this text, effective stress management and problem-solving strategies will be described which provide healthier alternatives to the above.

NONWORK STRESSORS

It is clear that distress emanating from outside the work situation will also impinge on work performance, satisfaction with work, and the therapist's emotional state while working. For example, a therapist who has had a serious argument with her partner prior to leaving home is likely to be still preoccupied and experiencing negative emotions during her first therapy session at the office, probably to the detriment of the session. The client may also sense something being different with the therapist and may struggle to interpret this change with possible negative consequences. The problem is not the fact that outside stressors occur and impact work, which is to be expected, but lays in the therapist's own expectation that she should be superhuman and the outside world can just be switched off upon arrival at work. A more realistic and healthy expectation may be that, at best, it will be possible to manage this stress and minimize the impairment involved. Another example illustrates the problem of unrealistic self-expectations set by therapists. A counselor, a former colleague of mine, did not feel that it was appropriate to cancel her afternoon therapy sessions after she heard at lunchtime of her mother's sudden death. Clearly, she was placing an unrealistic demand on herself. It seems obvious that the quality of therapy performed under these circumstances would be diminished in addition to being an occasion for further distress for the therapist concerned.

One useful way to examine the degree of stress experienced by therapy clients and its potential impact is to use a measure such as the Holmes and Rahe Social Readjustment Scale (Holmes & Rahe, 1967). This measure can also be used to monitor recent life events (such as the death of a spouse, divorce, marital separation, personal injury/illness, or change in health status of a close family member) experienced by, and having an impact on, a therapist. A therapist who has recently experienced any of these life events will probably struggle to cope with current work stressors, which previously may not have been a problem. The experience of one or more of these stressful major life events is likely to reduce the ability to manage daily demands and may compromise work performance to some extent. Even when stressors are not of the magnitude of these major life events, an accumulation of minor stressors may also have the effect of lowering the individual's threshold for dealing with work-related stressors. The Hassles Scale (Kanner et al., 1987) is a useful measure of the presence of many minor stresses (noise in the home environment, responsibility overload, too many interruptions, home maintenance problems, or rising prices) which can accumulate with detrimental effects on individuals experiencing them. Therapists, who are dealing with many of these, may find that their reactions to therapy and other work-related incidents change in the direction of more frequent negative emotional reactions. Stressors and pressure from outside work may also set up a vicious cycle of distress where individuals may try to compensate for home problems at work and vice versa, which leads to further problems. As mentioned previously, stressors may have a cumulative effect on therapists or mental health practitioners. For example, an individual who has coped well to date with certain home problems (financial strain and a child in trouble at school) may become overwhelmed and unable to cope when extra stressors that occur at work (job restructuring, criticism from a colleague or supervisor, and an increased case load). Realistically, therapists cannot, and should not, expect themselves to leave these stressors at the door when they come to work. However, they may be able to learn more effective strategies for reducing their impact, develop resilience, and ensure "damage limitation."

TRAINING INADEQUACIES

While engaged in postdoctoral training some years ago, I was pleased to see that a training workshop (on therapist dysfunctional reactions and how to manage them) had been scheduled. I realized that this was the first time in over 8 years of training in clinical psychology that such a workshop had been offered to me, and my fellow trainees had had the same experience. Over many subsequent years of surveying supervisees and trainees, I have found that training courses continue to pay little or no attention to this issue of psychotherapists dealing with their own emotions, thoughts, and behaviors, triggered by therapy situations. Since more and more CBT texts devote time and attention to challenging cases (e.g., A. T. Beck et al., 2003; J. S. Beck, 2005; Layden et al., 1993; Leahy, 2001), it could be argued that clinical and professional training courses should also focus more on these issues. In examining workshops and seminars presented at national mental health conferences, this topic is usually conspicuous by its absence. As a result of this and the lack of attention given to this topic in training, one is left with the idea that therapist distress is really not a problem or is a low priority issue. Consequently, any therapist experiencing some of the problems outlined in this text may well be ashamed or embarrassed to talk about these issues or ask for help or support and may end up believing (falsely) that no one else feels this way.

In the concluding parts of this text, some suggestions will be made for institutional changes that would help with the problem of inadequate training and lack of agency support in dealing with these issues. At this point, it could be said that individuals in charge of organizing or providing clinical training or supervision for professionals who deal with mental health clients should prioritize this issue. In supervising therapists, I tend to focus on supervisees' emotional statuses, vis-à-vis certain challenging cases, as well as helping them develop better conceptualization and intervention skills. It is obvious that a supervisee's emotional reactions will affect the degree to which these supervisee's therapeutic endeavors are likely to be effective. A recent study of therapists in supervision during Cognitive Therapy training found that the trainees' ratings of their own competence was influenced strongly by their emotional state and stress levels (Bennett-Levy & Beedie, 2007). In addition, the type of supervision described above, which focuses on both client issues and the therapist's reactions, can greatly reduce personal work-related stress as well as fine-tune therapists' clinical skills.

LACK OF ORGANIZATIONAL SUPPORT

Case supervision within an agency is often set up only to meet the requirements of the state or the agency itself. It is rare for an agency to routinely make peer, group, or individual supervision available for therapists dealing with difficult or challenging cases. Yet this would be time well spent and, most likely, be cost-effective in that it would probably improve client outcomes. In addition, it would show recognition of the distress and strain experienced by staff members, which would lead to a greater sense of being appreciated amongst mental health providers and increase worker satisfaction. Administrative support might come in the form of setting up supervision and staffing; sending individuals to training sessions on this topic; or bringing in speakers to provide onsite, staff-wide training in some of these issues. Additionally, organizing staff retreats — with workshops focusing not on learning more about certain disorders and therapy procedures, but rather on helping employees themselves by providing stress-reducing activities in a relaxing setting — would be conducive to distress-reduction. Regrettably, in many mental health agencies staff members are often so overloaded with clients and mandatory meetings that there is no time for the type of support activities outlined here, and this can be a recipe for burnout and distress. In private practice, where a therapist is paid only for billable hours involving client contact, it may be a low priority to organize something like the above; but the benefits of having even occasional staffing/supervision sessions with colleagues inside or outside the practice, as a means of dealing with some of these issues, should not be overlooked.

CBT STRATEGIES TO REDUCE THERAPIST DISTRESS

Cognitive behavioral strategies, which therapists can use as self-therapy during specific occurrences of distress in the course of their clinical practice, have been described by several writers in the field. J. S. Beck (2005) describes a method of carrying out emotional self-scanning when working with personality-disordered clients and challenging cases. By such means therapists can develop skills in detecting a change in their thinking, emotions, behavior, or physiology, which can cue them to the presence of a relational or other problem in therapy. For example, it is suggested that a simple way of monitoring the presence of any negative reactions to clients is for the therapist to check what thoughts and feelings emerge when he or she reviews the client appointment list for the day. Feelings of discomfort in anticipation of seeing someone or hoping that a particular client may cancel is an index of some negative feelings and associated distressing thoughts regarding treating or working with some individuals. J. S. Beck then goes on to demonstrate how the therapist can modify these feelings and thoughts by questioning their validity, looking for distortions in thinking, and using other cognitive techniques. Therapists working with very challenging cases are encouraged, on an ongoing basis, to identify their emotional reactions by asking themselves questions such as:

- Am I feeling any negative reactions such as anger, irritation, hopelessness, anxiety?
- Am I engaging in any dysfunctional behaviors such as blaming, demeaning, or controlling my client?
- What predictions am I making concerning how this client will behave in today's session?

If this monitoring of possible dysfunctional reactions reveals problems, then the therapist clearly needs to intervene to reduce his or her own distress and increase his or her effectiveness as a therapist, as this will in all probability be diminished by having such reactions. Similarly, Leahy (2001) suggests that therapists pay close attention to distortions that may arise in their thinking about themselves or their clients. For example, recognizing the thought that "Last week's progress with this client was just an illusion" is an example of a particular cognitive distortion (Disqualifying the Positive), will lead to more balanced, adaptive, and functional thinking concerning the therapeutic issues with a client whose progress is fluctuating. Layden et al. (1993) describe the steps a therapist, working with Borderline Personality Disorder clients, might take to alleviate their own dysfunctional thoughts and feelings of distress (which are often elicited by issues arising from the treatment of these individuals). A self-therapy strategy they recommend is for the therapist to fill out a Dysfunctional Thought Record (DTR) in the same way that clients are instructed to fill these out when experiencing depression or other negative emotions. On this form the therapist might record situations, feelings, thoughts, and behavioral responses when an impasse or problem occurs with a client. This procedure will be described in some detail later. Additionally, they advocate that the therapist do some cognitive rehearsal before any sessions which he or she predicts will be taxing or difficult.

Cognitive behavioral therapy writers have also stressed the importance of therapists establishing more functional belief systems (which foster a coping or problem-solving set) rather than a blaming attitude (which involves scapegoating either oneself or the client for the problems experienced in therapy). Lastly, it is has been suggested that some limited self-disclosure, where the therapist shares some of his or her feelings of frustration or anxiety, may be therapeutic for both the therapist and client, provided this is done carefully and with consideration of the possible consequences.

Historically, cognitive behavioral therapists have tended to avoid terms like transference and countertransference, as these two terms are linked with the psychoanalytic tradition. However, in dealing with complex and challenging cases, relationship factors are even more important than in more standard applications of Cognitive Behavior Therapy. When working with personality-disordered clients this may, of necessity, become a major therapeutic focus (A. T. Beck et al., 2003;

Layden et al., 1993). The therapist may need to look for schemas and belief systems, possibly acquired in childhood or early experiences, which are being activated by the therapy relationship. This can help explain many therapy-interfering behaviors on the part of the client, and can prevent the build-up of frustration with the client on the part of the therapist. Further, as Leahy (2001) suggests, it is important for therapists to understand also how their own schemas and belief systems may create a vulnerability that makes it more likely that they will be upset by certain situations, which are logically linked to this vulnerability. It can be instructive for therapists to ask themselves questions such as:

- Which kind of clients or client situations tend to create strong feelings in me?
- Which kinds of problems in therapy lead to nontherapeutic behaviors on my part?
- Which clients feel like friends and are hard to confront?

Having established what some of these "hot spots" are, the next step is to try to determine what the core beliefs or schemas are, which are activated by these situations, and where these come from. Another way of identifying these beliefs, Leahy (2001) suggests, is by the therapist asking himself or herself:

- What is my worst fear concerning a negative outcome in therapy (being sued, failing, being attacked)?
- If this did happen, what would it mean about me? (I am a failure, I am vulnerable.)
- How does the client situation and my beliefs and behaviors fit together? (If the client acts out, I should not confront him, as he may leave therapy and I will then have failed.)

The idea of therapists using the same techniques on themselves (which is effective in reducing distress in clients) is not new. More than 25 years ago, Albert Ellis (Ellis, 1983), one of the pioneers in the evolution of CBT, described some general principles for dealing with emotional disturbance arising out of therapeutic work. He encouraged therapists to:

- Identify irrational beliefs lying behind therapeutic upsets, especially those that contained absolutistic thinking (e.g., "I should be able to help everyone I see").
- Consider these as hypotheses to test and challenge.
- Review disconfirming evidence.
- Create alternative, rational, preferential statements (e.g., "I would like to help all my clients")
- Make self-acceptance nonconditional on therapeutic success or being liked by clients.
- Refuse to "awfulize" about things which are challenging (e.g., a client not doing homework is annoying or inconvenient rather than terrible).
- Persistently act against these irrational beliefs (e.g., tell oneself that, in fact, obnoxious behavior can actually be tolerated, despite the prediction that it cannot).

GENERAL GUIDELINES FOR THERAPISTS
WHO WORK WITH CHALLENGING CASES

Before proceeding to detailed descriptions of specific CBT interventions to deal with emotional reactions, which are distressing and counterproductive in therapy, some general suggestions will be offered for working with challenging cases as these are most likely to elicit therapist distress.

- Maintain a problem-solving attitude. Even when faced with obstacles try to remain calm, collaboratively attempt to identify what is interfering with progress, generate alternative solutions, and adopt a plan.
- When an impasse occurs, do not attribute responsibility for this to either the client or to yourself but see it as a problem to be solved and attempt to generate possible solutions.
- Avoid labeling or stereotyping the client. Instead, try to use the client case conceptualization to understand what is going on. For example, look at how what seems like "resistance" fits in with the client's beliefs and individual history.
- Identify and deal with any therapist dysfunctional cognitions. Methods to facilitate this will be described later.

- Be realistic in your expectations. Avoid the trap of thinking that no one will ever relapse, have setbacks, or not show a good response to the application of techniques that usually prove helpful to other clients. In addition, do not expect linear progress. It is more likely to be in a somewhat jig-jag fashion with stops and starts, even when the client is improving overall.
- Try to remain guardedly optimistic. Hopelessness, cynicism, or pessimism in the therapist will interfere with therapeutic progress just as these attitudes in the client can impair therapy. The therapist should promote the idea that some change in some facets of the client's functioning is always possible and communicate this to the client without creating false or irrational expectations.
- Maintain a high level of tolerance for frustration. Therapists working with challenging cases should expect and be prepared for roadblocks and frustration. A comprehensive case formulation should allow a prediction of what difficulties are likely to come up in the therapy itself or in the therapy relationship, based on the client's beliefs and compensatory strategies arising in part out of previous learning experiences. Being forewarned in this way, the therapist may be able to plan in advance for these problems and adapt the delivery of therapy accordingly.
- Avoid direct interpretations of clients' behavior. A questioning style is likely to elicit more information as well as facilitate therapeutic collaboration. Interpretations may lead to power battles and attempts by the client to either deny problems or argue against the therapist's overly directive or confrontational statements.
- Avoid buying into the client's distortions. Even when a client's situation is realistically "bad," it is important, while acknowledging this reality, to also examine the possible mediating influence of negative thinking or inadequate coping in "making a bad situation worse."
- Resist the urge to switch models when the going gets tough. It is possible to creatively interweave therapeutic interventions from other models or approaches, while still being guided by the original model or case conceptualization. The formulation can be extended in the light of new information and tested out by using additional interventions, but the unsystematic

applications of a range of techniques or models is likely to be ineffective and possibly confusing and antitherapeutic for the client.

- Do not expect or believe that you will have all the answers to every problem. It sometimes "goes against the grain" for some therapists, who have unrealistic expectations for themselves, to say to a client "I am not sure what the answer is but I will try and find out by consulting with colleagues or the literature." This may model for the client effective problem solving with the absence of a demand on you to be perfect or all-competent.

In the next pages, specific step-by-step interventions will be described that can help therapists with episodes of distress triggered by specific therapy events.

SPECIFIC CBT INTERVENTIONS

RECOGNIZING EARLY WARNING SIGNALS

As alluded to earlier, it is important to detect early warning signals of stress or distress before they become severe and impairing. This could be likened to paying attention to the yellow gas light on one's dashboard, which, if ignored, can lead to serious consequences. Therapists may not always be the best at detecting subtle distress reactions, which can be a prequel to more serious problems.

A helpful exercise is for therapists to periodically review the following list, referred to in an earlier section, to determine if any of these tell-tale signs are evident.

- Frequently feeling tired
- Arguing with others over minor things
- Never being able to relax
- Constantly feeling in demand or under pressure
- Lacking patience or tolerance
- Feeling there is not enough time for yourself, family, or friends
- Memory and concentration lapses
- Lacking interest in or time for socializing or engaging in recreational activities

- Feeling irritable, tired, and unfulfilled at the end of the work day

In addition, the following exercise can be helpful. Completing the form on the next page will help the therapist to identify characteristic stress markers that can then be regularly monitored to allow early intervention.

Personal Indicators of Distress

Specify below changes you have noticed during periods of stress in the following areas:

1. **Changes in my behavior** (e.g., irritability, withdrawal from others, lack of productivity)

    Specify: _____

    _____

    _____

    _____

    _____

    _____

    _____

2. **Changes in my body** (e.g., sleep problems, eating disturbances, headaches, tiredness)

    Specify: _____

    _____

    _____

    _____

    _____

    _____

3. **Changes in my thinking** (e.g., poor concentration, indecisiveness, pessimism, self-blame)

    Specify: _____

    _____

    _____

    _____

    _____

4. Changes in me that other people who know me well have commented on or brought to my attention (e.g., friends or family say that I am snappy or that I become distant or withdrawn)

Specify: _____

_____

_____

_____

_____

_____

_____

IDENTIFYING CHARACTERISTIC STRESSORS

It can also be very helpful to identify relevant situational triggers or "stress buttons," which are likely to occur in the therapist's work situation. These will often be specific to a particular individual and in all probability likely to be influenced by personal characteristics, belief systems, and expectations. Identifying high-risk situations for lapse/relapse or the emergence of problems has considerable therapeutic benefit for a wide range of clients, as it allows planning and preparing in advance for these challenges. Likewise, a therapist, from his or her own past responses, can learn to identify clinical or nonclinical situations in his or her practice that can elicit certain stress reactions. This will be enormously helpful in taking steps to combat and deal with these trigger events more effectively.

In the following exercise, it may be helpful for a therapist to identify situations which have the potential to elicit distress responses for him.

What are Some Stressors/Triggers
That Stress/Distress Me in the Workplace?

Client-Related Stressors/Triggers

Specify: _____

_____

_____

_____

_____

_____

_____

_____

Administrative/Organizational Stressors/Triggers

Specify: _____

_____

_____

_____

_____

_____

_____

_____

Other Stressors/Triggers

Specify: _____

_____

_____

_____

_____

_____

_____

_____

IDENTIFYING DYSFUNCTIONAL THINKING

The steps outlined in the next section (to identify negative thoughts and beliefs) will be familiar to counselors who use Cognitive Behavior Therapy in their practice. However, they may not have used these methods to carefully examine their own emotional reactions. This systematic approach can be easily and effectively implemented in episodes of distress or emotional upset at work by asking themselves the following questions:

- Question 1. Is there a noticeable shift in feelings experienced (an onset of distress or upset)?
- Question 2. What are the specific emotions experienced and what is the intensity of each on a 0 to 100 scale?
- Question 3. What is the situation eliciting the distressing emotions (the trigger event)?
- Question 4. What are the relevant thoughts and beliefs about this situation that influence the emotions or feelings experienced?

At this point the therapist should be able to identify examples of:

- An emotion (anger, irritation, sadness, anxiety) and its intensity (0-100)
- A trigger situation (client behavior, therapy impasse, non-client-related problem)
- Automatic thoughts linking the situation and the emotion

To take an example, imagine the following scenario:

You notice that during a session your emotional state has changed (Question 1) and you are becoming anxious (Question 2). This emotion has an intensity of 70 on a 0 to 100 scale (Question 2). You started to become anxious as the client began talking about how frustrated he feels that he is no better after 6 weeks of therapy (Question 3). You catch yourself thinking, "What if he drops out of therapy or what if he is so demoralized that he becomes actively suicidal?" (Question 4).

This is a clear example of the CBT model with a situation (the client stating that he is frustrated) leading to specific automatic thoughts ("What if he drops out of therapy or becomes actively suicidal?") leading to emotions (anxiety). Having established this connection, the next step is to test and challenge the identified thoughts.

It may be helpful to practice this step (identifying the situation-thoughts-feelings link) in the following two exercises.

Imagine the following scenarios:

Situation 1. Despite your best efforts, a client gives you the following feedback: "You don't really seem to care what happens to me. You don't have any problems and so can't understand what I am going through. I am just a way that you make a living and am not of any importance to you."

How might you feel? What emotions might be triggered by this? What thoughts might you have concerning what the client said? What meaning might this have for you?

Situation 2. You have just heard from the hospital admissions department that a client you see (who has been doing well) has had a relapse, is severely depressed, and is being hospitalized with suicidal ideation.

How might you feel? What emotions might be triggered by this? What thoughts might you have concerning this? What meaning might this have for you?

Situation 3. You have a full case load and are feeling pressured and stressed. Your agency director tells you that, due to cutbacks, you will have to see some extra clients one evening a week.

How might you feel? What emotions might be triggered by this? What thoughts might you have? What meaning might this have for you?

In the above examples it may become evident how situations, thoughts, and feelings interact. In addition, the mediating role which certain thoughts play in creating negative feelings may also be clearly seen.

Another useful thought identification method is for a therapist to **retrospectively** focus on a recent time doing therapy when feelings of frustration, anxiety, or irritation occurred. For example, one could recall an episode where some distress related to a client was experienced. Identifying the situation and emotion, as on the form on the next page, can be facilitated by asking the questions listed below:

- What was the situation?
- What happened?
- What feelings did I have?
- What thoughts did I have?
- What was going through my mind when I began to feel upset in this situation?
- What meaning did it have for me?
- Why was it a problem?

The form on the next page is a useful way of **prospectively** identifying the components of an episode of distress occurring in a work situation by allowing the therapist to systematically examine the different components of the problem, including the situation, associated thoughts, and subsequent feelings. With this information the therapist can then proceed to thought-challenging or other self-directed interventions which will now be described.

Identifying Thoughts

Feelings	Situation	Thoughts
Rate Intensity (0-100)	Where were you? What was going on?	What went through your mind?

IDENTIFYING THE EFFECTS OF THINKING

Before proceeding to methods that test the validity of the thoughts and beliefs which underlie therapists' emotional reactions, it can be helpful to look at the effects that certain thoughts or thinking processes can have on the therapist in both the emotional and behavioral arena. This serves two purposes:

- It helps recognize how dysfunctional thinking can have significant effects on both the individual and on his or her clients.
- It provides a motivation to test and revise this thinking to a more healthy and functional set of cognitions.

The steps involved are as follows:

- Take an identified thought from an analysis of the thoughts involved when negative feelings are elicited by a therapy situation. Examples might be "This patient doesn't want to get better" or "He is deliberately sabotaging my efforts."
- Ask the following questions:
  o What is the effect on me of having these thoughts?
  o What effect does it have on my emotions?
  o What effect does it have on my behavior within therapy and outside?

It may become obvious that these thoughts probably lead to irritation and frustration (emotional consequences) and may also result in working less hard with this client, being defensive, and acting in an irritated manner, which may in turn influence the client's actions (behavioral consequences).

- Following the analysis above, the next step is to check out the validity of these thoughts by using standard CBT techniques.

In doing this kind of functional analysis, the costs and benefits of having certain thoughts and beliefs (about oneself, the client, or the therapy) can be examined. The form on the next page may facilitate the process of carrying out this procedure systematically.

Analyzing the Effects of Thoughts/Beliefs

Identified thought/belief:

_____

_____

_____

_____

_____

_____

_____

Degree of belief (0-100%) _____

Advantages of Holding This Belief	Disadvantages of Holding This Belief
How does it help me?	How does it hinder me?

IDENTIFYING DISTORTIONS

In the same manner that identifying distortions in thinking can help clients distance themselves from their thinking and begin reappraising their thoughts, the ability to recognize distorted thinking can also be very beneficial for therapists.

The steps involved are as follows:

- Become familiar with the concept of cognitive distortions by reading the handout "Cognitive Distortions (Nine Ways to Make Yourself Miserable)" on the next page.
- Identify any tendencies to engage in any particular distortions by supplying some personal examples as suggested in this handout.
- Examine an identified thought or set of thoughts collected from a recent upsetting situation and recorded on the previous Identifying Thoughts form in the light of these descriptions and criteria.
- Label which distortion(s), if any, is in evidence in this thought or set of thoughts. For example, having the thought "The client does not want to get better and is sabotaging me and the therapy" is an example of Labeling and Personalizing (Blaming). The thought that "I am not doing good therapy and this client will relapse" is an example of Jumping to Conclusions (Fortune Telling and Mental Filter).
- Respond to the initial dysfunctional thought(s) that will follow logically from the detection of distortions.

After the steps above, the therapist might now replace the initial dysfunctional thought with an alternative cognitive response such as "I will try to think of how to make this therapy more effective rather than blame myself, but in any case, what happens in the future for the client is unknown and not entirely in my control," which is likely to be more helpful and functional.

The "Recognizing Distortions in Thinking" form on page 61 can be used to record problem situations, feelings, thoughts, and distortions as a means to facilitate cognitive reappraisal and reframing.

Cognitive Distortions
(Nine Ways to Make Yourself Miserable)

Cognitive distortions are inaccuracies in our thinking. We can think of our thoughts as representations of reality, sort of like a photograph. If we have a smudge on the lens of the camera, then the photo will show a picture which does not accurately represent what was in front of the camera. Even if the lens is clear and we take a picture of only part of an object, then the picture will not accurately portray the whole object. It is safe to assume that everyone has cognitive distortions.

Please do not assume that you are hopelessly defective if you recognize some or all of those that are described below. It can be very helpful to be able to identify distortions in our thinking because once we have discovered the distortion, we will know how to correct it and feel better. Identifying our cognitive distortions is like diagnosing the thought problem. A good diagnosis usually points to a helpful remedy.

Below is a list of nine common distortions with examples of how they might occur. See if you can identify one or more ways that you have been victimized by this kind of thinking.

1. **All or Nothing/Black or White:** Seeing things as though they were only two possible categories.

    Example: If a situation turns out imperfectly, you see it as a total failure. You forget to buy one item on a shopping list and think "Well, I really blew that trip." Can you think of an example of how you have used this distortion? Try writing it down below.

    _____

    _____

    _____

    _____

    _____

    _____

2. **Overgeneralizing:** A negative event is seen as a never-ending pattern of defeat.

Example: When shopping you notice that your check-out line is moving very slowly and think, "Why do I always pick the slowest line?" Your example:

_____

_____

_____

_____

3. **Mental Filter:** Seeing only negative aspects of a situation while screening out the positive aspects.

Example: You focus on a critical comment someone made while ignoring all the compliments you received. Your example:

_____

_____

_____

_____

4. **Jumping to Conclusions:** Predicting things will go a certain way before you have the facts.

a. Mind Reading: Assuming that you know exactly what someone is or will be thinking about you.

Example: An acquaintance doesn't seem as friendly as usual and you think, "He must be angry with me." Your example:

_____

_____

_____

b. Fortune Telling: Predicting that things will turn out badly and that you won't be able to cope.

Example: Before going to a social gathering, you have an image of people reacting negatively to you and you assume that you will be devastated. Your example:

_____

_____

_____

5. **Magnifying or Minimizing:** Overevaluating or minimizing the importance of a situation or certain information.

    Example: Even though you may be a good parent and spouse, you think that it's shameful to have been laid off from a job. You get several job offers and accept one but think that it doesn't make up for the loss. Your example:

    _____
    _____
    _____
    _____
    _____

6. **Emotional Reasoning:** Assuming that how you feel is an accurate reflection of how things are.

    Example: If you are feeling anxious, you assume that something bad is going to happen. Your Example:

    _____
    _____
    _____
    _____
    _____

7. **Shoulds:** You tell yourself things "should" or "shouldn't" be a certain way. We do this with ourselves, with other people, and situations. Variations of this can include "musts," "have to's," and other imperatives which sound like they come from some authority figure.

    Example: "You have to help me," or "I shouldn't have done that." Your example:

    _____
    _____
    _____
    _____
    _____

8. **Labeling:** This is an extreme form of all-or-nothing thinking which can be damaging to our self-esteem and our relationships. Instead of simply acknowledging a mistake, we say, "I'm such a screw-up" (substitute "loser," "idiot," "jerk," etc.). Applying labels, "that SOB," will tend to blind us to other qualities which we or others have.

   Everyone has their favorites. What are yours?

   _____

   _____

   _____

   _____

   _____

9. **Personalizing:** (Blaming) This distortion creates enormous preventable suffering. This occurs when we hold ourselves responsible for something which isn't or wasn't entirely under our control. As children, we personalize much of what happens around us including how we are treated. When a child is mistreated by a parent, she will tend to assume that she is somehow to blame and will see herself as defective. We do this as adults, often without realizing it. Now we have a choice when we become aware of this destructive distortion. Most importantly, we can change it! When this process is reversed, we blame someone else entirely for a situation we have a part in creating.

   Example: The same person who noticed the friend who didn't seem as friendly as usual thought, "I must have done something wrong." Your example:

   _____

   _____

   _____

   _____

   _____

Recognizing Distortions in Thinking

Feelings	Situation	Thoughts	Distortions
Rate Intensity 0-100	Where were you? What was going on?	What went through your mind?	Identify the distortion for each thought.

TESTING THE EVIDENCE

Therapists can reality-test their automatic thoughts (when they involve assumptions or general conclusions) by using the method described below. The steps involved are as follows:

- Identify the exact conclusion or assumption being made (e.g., the assumption that "I am an inadequate therapist" elicited by a client relapsing or having a setback).
- Define the terms involved (in the example above, it may be important to know what would define an "adequate" or a "more than adequate" therapist). This step may reveal unrealistic expectations the individual has for himself or herself.
- Ask the question what the level of belief in the thought is on a 0 to 100 belief scale. The importance of this step is that low-belief ratings can kick-start the process of seeing the other side (reasons why this is thought is not valid or accurate). Also, this is a good baseline against which to later reassess the believability of these initial thoughts.
- List all the evidence which supports the assumption. In the above example, the data (which, of course, can subsequently be critically reviewed) might include specific clients who have not done well or other indices of inadequate therapy.
- List evidence which goes against the assumption. In this same example, this might include clients who have reported positive outcomes as well as any positive feedback received from referral agents and colleagues.
- Reconsider the original assumption and how much it is now believed. This cognitive intervention will often successfully challenge the overgeneralized responding which occurs when an event is taken out of context.
- Decide if any further action is needed to test out the assumption or initial negative thought. For example, clients' feedback can be elicited regarding their satisfaction with therapy .

The form on the next page can be a very useful and systematic way of carrying out this kind of cognitive intervention.

Reviewing the Evidence

Identified thought:

_____

_____

_____

_____

_____

Degree of belief (0-100%) _____

Evidence for	Evidence against

Degree of belief in thought now (0-100%): _____

Action plan to further test the thought: _____

_____

_____

_____

_____

_____

_____

_____

_____

_____

_____

_____

_____

_____

_____

_____

_____

_____

_____

_____

_____

_____

_____

_____

GENERATING ALTERNATIVE VIEWPOINTS

This technique, also known as reattribution, can be helpful in evaluating negative, rigid, and emotionally arousing explanations of events by considering other less negative interpretations. The steps involved are as follows:

- Identify exactly how a stressful situation is being interpreted and what effect this interpretation is having. An example is a situation where a client is having a setback or lapse and this is seen as a reflection of the therapist not being competent enough. This interpretation demoralizes the therapist to the extent that both this client's therapy and therapy in general is rendered less effective.
- Brainstorm all other possible explanations for this event. In the above example, looking at other factors which might have contributed to the event (the setback/lapse) might bring to light the fact that the client missed several doses of his psychotropic medication, has had a lot of extra recent stress, was demoralized, and was not following the plan discussed for how to deal with setbacks.
- Review the evidence to support each of these alternatives and estimate how likely it is that each contributed to the outcome.
- Come up with a more sophisticated and comprehensive explanation for what happened based on the above.
- Problem solve what can be done to address these issues. In the above example, possible solutions may include facilitating greater client compliance with medication and psychotherapy, targeting the additional stress, working on the demoralization cognitively, and checking into other therapeutic interventions in addition to what has already been implemented.

The form on the next page may be helpful in facilitating the use of this cognitive technique.

Generating Alternatives

Identified thought:

_____

_____

_____

_____

_____

_____

Degree of belief (0-100%) _____

List All Other Possible Viewpoints or Explanations	What is the Evidence for This?

Degree of belief in original thought now (0-100%): _____

Is more information needed to decide which of the above is more likely or logical?   ☐ Yes   ☐ No

If so, how could this be obtained?

Action plan: _____

_____

_____

_____

_____

_____

_____

_____

_____

_____

_____

_____

_____

_____

_____

_____

_____

_____

_____

_____

_____

_____

_____

DECATASTROPHIZING AND DE-AWFULIZING

If the thoughts identified in the analysis of distressing situations described previously involves some "what if" or "worst case scenario" thinking, this technique can help to (a) more realistically assess how likely this scenario actually is, and (b) consider how bad the consequences would be, if they did actually happen. The steps involved are as follows:

- Identify what negative outcomes are being predicted. For example, after meeting a new therapy client and suspecting the diagnosis might be Borderline Personality Disorder, the therapist may note the following automatic thoughts (linked with negative emotions) occurring: "This will be draining, she will be manipulative, suicidal, demanding, and angry, and I won't be able to do effective therapy."
- Consider how likely it is that each of these will actually occur (decatastrophizing). In the above example, the therapist might have the following re-appraisal: "In my experience, not all Borderline clients act this way. I can recall some who didn't. How likely is it, both from the research and from my prior experience, that I won't be able to be effective to some extent in some areas?"
- Consider the worst outcome and what the consequences would be (de-awfulizing). How awful would it actually be if that did happen? What coping strategies could be used to deal with this? In the example above, the therapist might ask himself or herself: "Even if this client does act in all these ways, what then? How would I handle it therapeutically and personally?"
- "Even if I couldn't do standard therapy, what could I do?"
- By reviewing the above, it often becomes apparent that the individual might be assuming the worst (which may not happen) and, even if it did, he or she actually has a number of resources to effectively deal with it. This will lead to a reduction in emotional distress .

The form on the next page may help to explore the probabilities and consequences of negative predictions. Filling it out systematically, when these situations come up, may facilitate both decatastrophizing and de-awfulizing.

Decatastrophizing

My worst fear	How likely is this? (0-100%)	What would I do if it did happen? How would I cope?	What is the most likely outcome?

PUTTING IT ALL TOGETHER (ADAPT)

All or some of the techniques which have been outlined in this section may prove to be helpful when a therapist is experiencing strong emotional or cognitive reactions which are associated with impairment in the emotional or behavioral arenas.

A quick useful method of dealing with an episode of emotional distress, when conducting therapy or more generally in the work place, is represented in the following procedure. This method, contained in the acronym ADAPT, is described below. It summarizes the key steps a therapist (or client) can use in applying CBT in a way which facilitates self-help.

The acronym ADAPT stands for **A**ctivating events and triggers, **D**etecting feelings and thoughts, **A**nswering thoughts, **P**roceeding adaptively, and **T**esting the outcome.

The ADAPT questionnaire is on the following two pages.

ADAPT
Questionnaire

Using this brief Cognitive Behavioral procedure for episodes of workplace distress involves the following:

1. **Activating event or trigger**

   What is the stressful situation?
   Specify_____

   _____

2. **Detecting feelings and thoughts**

   What are my emotions?
   Specify_____

   _____

   What are my physical feelings?
   Specify_____

   _____

   What are my key thoughts and beliefs relating to this situation?
   Specify_____

   _____

   What is the effect of my thinking on my emotions and behavior?
   Specify_____

   _____

3. **Answering thoughts**

   What is the evidence for and against my thoughts?
   Specify (for)_____

   _____

   Specify (against) _____

   _____

What is another way I could look at this?
Specify_____

_____

What is the worst that could happen and how likely is this?
Specify_____

_____

What would I do if the worst did happen?
Specify_____

_____

4. **Proceeding adaptively**

What can I do or how can I think that will help me deal more effectively with this present situation?
Specify_____

_____

What can I do in general to reduce my current level of distress?
Specify_____

_____

5. **Testing the outcome**

What has changed in how I am feeling or how I am acting since coming up with or proceeding with the plan noted above? Is it working?
Specify_____

_____

GENERAL GUIDELINES FOR DISTRESS
REDUCTION IN THE WORKPLACE

There are a number of books that offer suggestions on effectively dealing with stress in the workplace (Farber, 1983; Klareich, 1990; Kottler, 1999; Lederer & Hall, 1999). These incorporate strategies and interventions based on cognitive behavioral and related approaches. Drawing on these sources and also utilizing ideas presented at the author's seminars on Reducing Stress in Mental Health Professionals, the following suggestions are offered for those dealing with the distress involved in working as a mental health treatment provider:

- Watch for early signs of distress and take action as early as possible.
- Identify any external stressors. Reduce these sources of distress when possible or alternately develop effective coping skills when they cannot be reduced.
- In each episode of distress, consider the contribution made by (a) the situation itself, and (b) the associated thoughts or thinking style in creating the distress reaction.
- Define concretely the problem(s) involved. Dismantle the problem into the components of situations, thoughts, and feelings.
- Check out and deal with any dysfunctional cognitions identified.
- Become an effective problem solver by brainstorming all possible solutions, evaluating the pros and cons of each, selecting the most feasible, putting this into action, and reviewing the results.
- Do not make self-esteem contingent on work or work performance.
- Keep things in perspective and avoid catastrophizing.
- Make sure not to personalize negative events.
- Do not engage in overgeneralization, black or white thinking, or other cognitive distortions.
- Have realistic expectations and avoid the Messiah complex. Do not assume that one can be superman or superwoman.

- Set realistic, achievable goals for oneself and monitor progress towards these. Give oneself credit for achieving these and recognize small gains in a positive direction.
- Examine the role of personal behavior in maintaining or creating distress. Identify anything one is doing which makes a bad situation worse.
- Plan to reduce or eliminate self-defeating behaviors from one's repertoire. Look at the adaptiveness of the coping strategies currently being used.
  - Abandon any that create their own problems (e.g., drinking or overeating).
  - Substitute healthy stress management techniques (e.g., meditation, yoga, relaxation techniques, exercise, or visualization) for any unhealthy or destructive ones.
- Utilize a whole variety of "stress busters" (which may potentially work based on past experience) and current resources available. On the "Action Plan for Distress Management" form (pp. 76-77) list everything that can be done in the event of the onset or exacerbation of distress.
- Give up trying to control the behavior of others, because this is a set-up for frustration. It is important to realize that one can be an influence but not exert control over other people including clients, colleagues, family, and friends.
- Use humor and realize that events can always be seen from another (less serious) perspective. In particular, be willing and able to make fun of oneself (not the client) and in the process create an alternative view of the situation.
- Develop a personalized emotional fire drill. Plan in advance strategies that can be implemented at times of acute distress.
- Take a more compassionate attitude towards oneself. Act as one would towards a beloved friend or family member, giving the same support and encouragement.
- Look after oneself better in terms of rest, diet, and exercise.
- Create a variety of self-soothing or relaxing activities. Adjust the balance of life activities, if the ratio of pleasure to tasks (work or other tasks) is imbalanced. Come up with a list of past activities that used to be fun or relaxing, but now are done infrequently; or a list of activities that seem appealing to do and are feasible to initiate currently.

- Practice all the things that one teaches clients. This is captured in the adage "physician heal thyself."
- Use the same effective tools prescribed for clients to deal with one's own distress or problems.
- Realize when help is needed for oneself. Work on any negative thinking which interferes with this (e.g., "I shouldn't need help," "I should be in control of my feelings since I am trained in this field").
- Create a support system for oneself. Reach out to colleagues and others.
- Seek professional help, if this is appropriate. Actively dispute and challenge any shame and embarrassment (with associated negative thoughts) which might prevent this. Bear in mind that the kind of work therapists do make it more likely, rather than less, that they may need and benefit from professional help at times. This can be a valid and self-protective option if some of the other strategies above prove insufficient.

Action Plan For
Distress Management

List below all the things you could do to deal with your distress. The list can include anything you've done in the past which reduced your distress and any ideas that you have heard or read about which you think might be helpful.

1. _____

_____

_____

2. _____

_____

_____

3. _____

_____

_____

4. _____

_____

_____

5. _____

_____

_____

6. _____

_____

_____

7. _____

_____

_____

8. _____

_____

_____

9. _____
   _____
   _____

10. _____
    _____
    _____

11. _____
    _____
    _____

12. _____
    _____
    _____

ORGANIZATIONAL INTERVENTIONS

In addition to the above, there are a number of steps which those with administrative responsibility within organizations and agencies could take to reduce or prevent mental health worker stress/distress. These might include

- facilitating the setting up of support networks or peer supervision for therapists.
- implementing and supporting staff retreats geared both to staff renewal and to acquiring knowledge or skills to work more effectively with clients.
- providing a climate of appreciation and recognition of employees' efforts and dedication.
- increasing positive reinforcement/rewards, both social and material.
- organizing social events and outings as a means of recognizing the service given by employees
- restructuring work demands, where feasible.
- ensuring that there is an equitable distribution of the more challenging therapy cases.
- creating a supervision or staffing system for therapists working with challenging clients.
- involving staff in decisions regarding policy and the agency's mission or direction.
- providing an uplifting and comfortable physical working environment.
- ensuring that staff members feel comfortable in asking for help with client situations or other work issues.

A more detailed analysis of how organizations contribute to personal stress and steps to rectify or reduce this can be found in Mashlach and Leiter (1997) and Cooper and Williams (1994).

A FINAL WORD

Working in the field of mental health, and in particular providing therapy or counseling to mental health clients, can be a trigger for emotional distress with concomitant behavioral consequences. The role of dysfunctional cognitions in this process is key and therapists themselves are likely to benefit from utilizing the same cognitive behavioral techniques that have been found to be very effective with a range of psychiatric disorders. This text has aimed to give a conceptualization of therapist distress based on the influence of beliefs and cognitive processing on situations triggering emotional distress in therapists. Identifying these patterns of response can lead to modification of identified dysfunctional thinking and behavior, which will not only reduce levels of distress in therapists, but also in all probability, improve their therapeutic effectiveness as well.

It is my sincere wish that this text will be helpful for you, the readers, in a practical and immediate way. Good luck in your therapeutic work with your clients and especially with the most important of these — yourself!

REFERENCES

Beck, A. T., Freeman, A., Davis, D. D., and associates. (2006). *Cognitive Therapy of Personality Disorders* (2nd ed.). New York: Guilford.

Beck, A. T., Rush, A. J., Shaw, B. F., & Emery, G. (1979). *Cognitive Therapy of Depression.* New York: Guilford.

Beck, A. T., Freeman, A., & Davis, D. D. (2003). *Cognitive Therapy of Personality Disorders* (2nd ed.). New York: Guilford.

Beck, J. S. (2005). *Cognitive Therapy With Challenging Cases. What to do When the Basics Don't Work.* New York: Guilford.

Bennett-Levy, J., & Beedie, A. (2007). The ups and downs of cognitive therapy training: What happens to trainees' perceptions of their competence during a cognitive therapy training course. *Behavioural and Cognitive Psychotherapy, 35*(1), 61-75.

Butler, A., Chapman, J. E., Froman, E. M., & Beck, A. T. (2006). The empirical status of cognitive behavior therapy: A review of meta-analyses. *Clinical Psychology Review, 26,* 17-31.

Cooper, C. L., & Williams, S. (Eds.). (1994). *Creating Healthy Work Organizations.* London: John Wiley and Sons.

Cushway, D., & Tyler, P. (1994). Stress and coping in clinical psychologists. *Stress Medicine, 10,* 35-40.

Ellis, A. (1983). How to deal with your most difficult client - you. *Journal of Rational Emotive Therapy, 1,* 3-8.

Emery, G. (2000). *Overcoming Depression.* Oakland, CA: New Harbinger.

Evans, S., Huxley, P., Gately, C., Webber, M., Mears, A., Pajak, S., ... Katona, C. (2006). Mental health, burnout and job satisfaction among mental health social workers in England and Wales. *British Journal of Psychiatry, 188,* 75-80.

Farber, B. (Ed.). (1983). *Stress and Burnout in Human Service Professionals.* New York: Pergamon.

Figley, R. (2002). Compassion fatigue: Psychotherapists chronic lack of self care. *Journal of Clinical Psychology, 58,* 1433-1441.

Fisher, D., Houston, J., & Galloway, S. (2008). *Sexual Offenders and Mental Health: Multidisciplinary Management in the Community.* London: Jessica Kingsley.

Fortener, R. G. (1990). *Relationship between work setting, client prognosis, suicide ideation and burnout in psychologist and counselors* (Doctoral Dissertation). University of Toledo.

Grosch, W. N., & Olsen, D. C. (1994). *When Helping Starts to Hurt. A New Look at Burnout Among Psychotherapists.* New York: W.W. Norton.

Holmes, T., & Rahe, R. H. (1967). Holmes-Rahe Life Changes Scale. *Journal of Psychosomatic Reasearch, 11,* 213-218.

Kanner, A. D., Coyne, J. C., Schachter, C., & Lazarus, R. (1987). Comparison of two modes of stress management: Daily hassles and uplifts versus major life events. *Journal of Behavioral Medicine, 24,* 29.

Klareich, E. (1990). *Working Without Stress.* New York: Bruner-Mazel.

Koepping, L. (1998). Managing anxiety: The client's and mine. *Women and Therapy, 21*(3), 49-54.

Kottler, J. (1999). *The Therapist's Workbook: Self Assessment, Self Care, and Self Improvement Exercises for Mental Health Professionals.* San Francisco: Jossey-Bass.

LaCoursie, C. (2001). Burnout and substance user treatment: The phenomenon and the administrator-clinician experience. *Substance Use and Misuse, 36,* 1839-1874.

Layden, M. A., Newman, C. F., Freeman, A., & Morse, S. B. (1993). *Cognitive Therapy of Borderline Personality Disorder.* Boston: Allyn & Bacon.

Leahy, R. L.(2001). *Overcoming Resistance in CognitiveTherapy.* New York: Guilford.

Leahy, R. L. (Ed.). (2003). *Roadblocks in Cognitive-Behavioral Therapy: Transforming Challenges into Opportunities for Change.* New York: Guilford.

Lederer, D., & Hall, M. (1999). *Instant Relaxation: How to Reduce Stress at Work, at Home and in Your Daily Life.* London: Crown House.

Levinson, R. (1998). The client revisited: A second look at a near failure. *Women and Therapy, 21*(3) 55-61.

Mashlach, C. (1982). *Burnout: The Cost of Caring.* New York: Prentice Hall.

Maslach, C., & Leiter, M. P. (1997). *The Truth About Burnout: How Organizations Cause Personal Stress and What to Do About It.* San Francisico: Jossey-Bass.

Matsakis, A. (1998). *Managing Client Anger: What to do When a Client is Angry With You.* Oakland, CA: New Harbinger.

Miller, D. (2000). *Dying to Care: Work Stress and Burnout in HIV/ AIDS Professionals.* London: Routledge.

Miller, W. R., & Rollnick, S. (2002). *Motivational Interviewing: Preparing People for Change* (2nd ed.). New York: Guilford.

Moore, K. A., & Cooper, C. L. (1996). Stress in mental health professionals: A theoretical overview. *International Journal of Social Psychiatry, 42*(2), 82-89.

Onyett, S., Pillinger, T., & Muijen, M. (1997). Job satisfaction and burnout among members of community mental health teams. *Journal of Mental Health, 6*(1), 55-66.

Paradis, L. F. (1987). *Stress and Burnout Among Providers Caring for the Terminally Ill and Their Families.* New York: Haworth.

Prochaska, J. O., & DiClemente, C. C. (1984). *The Transtheoretical Approach: Crossing Traditional Boundaries of Therapy.* Homewood, IL: Dow Jones-Irwin.

Pines, A., & Maslach, C. (1978). Characteristics of staff burnout in mental health settings. *Hospital and Community Psychiatry, 29,* 233-237.

Rees, D. W., & Cooper, C. L. (1992). Occupational stress in health service employees. *Health Services Management Research, 3,* 163-172.

Ritchie, E. C., Watson, P. J., & Friedman, M. J. (2006). *Interventions Following Mass Violence and Disasters: Strategies for Mental Health Practice.* New York: Guilford.

Sedgewick, D. (1994). *The Wounded Healer: Countertransference From a Jungian Perspective.* London: Routledge.

Shinn, M., Rosario, M., March, H., & Chesnutt, D. E. (1984). Coping with job stress and burnout in the human services. *Journal of Personality and Social Psychology, 46,* 864-876.

Stamm, B. H. (2003). *Secondary Traumatic Stress: Self-care Issues for Clinicians, Researchers and Educators.* Eau Claire, WI: PESI Health Care.

Wells, A. (1997). *Cognitive Therapy of Anxiety Disorders: A Practice Manual and Conceptual Guide.* West Sussex, England: John Wiley & Sons.

Wilson, K. G. (2008). *Mindfulness for Two: An Acceptance and Commitment Therapy Approach to Mindfulness in Psychotherapy.* Oakland, CA: New Harbinger.